Mark Morris

Series Editors: Steve Barlow and Steve Skidmore

Published by Heinemann Educational Publishers
Halley Court, Jordan Hill, Oxford OX2 8EJ
A division of Reed Educational and Professional Publishing Ltd

OXFORD   MELBOURNE   AUCKLAND
JOHANNESBURG   BLANTYRE   GABORONE
IBADAN   PORTSMOUTH NH (USA)   CHICAGO

© Mark Morris, 2001
Original illustrations © Heinemann Educational Publishers 2001

All rights reserved. No part of this publication may be reproduced in any material form (including photocopying or storing it in any medium by electronic means and whether or not transiently or incidentally to some other use of this publication) without the prior written permission of the copyright owner, except in accordance with the provisions of the Copyright, Designs and Patents Act 1988 or under the terms of a licence issued by the Copyright Licensing Agency Ltd, 90 Tottenham Court Road, London W1P 0LP. Applications for the copyright owner's written permission to reproduce any part of this publication should be addressed in the first instance to the publisher.

05 04 03 02 01
10 9 8 7 6 5 4 3 2 1
ISBN 0 435 21490 X

Photographs: p.8 – Allsport; p.13 – Corbis; p.15 – Colorsport;
p.20 – Mirror Syndication; pp.27 and 30 – Popperfoto
Cover design by Shireen Nathoo Design
Cover artwork by Roger Langridge
Designed by Artistix, Thame, Oxon
Printed and bound in Great Britain by Biddles Ltd

Tel: 01865 888058   www.heinemann.co.uk

Contents

The best game in the world	5
Barmy beginnings	6
Record breakers	8
Ups and downs	11
Daft debuts	14
Potty players	16
Football families	19
Off you go!	20
Goofy goals	22
Stunning results	24
The greatest fightbacks ever?	28
Extra time	29
Crazy Quiz – Answers	32

The best game in the world

Football is the most popular game in the world. More people watch football than any other sport.

It is fast, exciting and full of action. The rules are easy. It is cheap to play. All you need is a ball!

Millions of people watch football all over the world. Some teams even have their own TV channels! Famous players can earn lots of money.

Lots of amazing things happen. Some are unusual. Some are fantastic. Some are just silly. This is why the world is 'football crazy'.

Barmy beginnings

Famous teams of today had to start somewhere…

- Many years ago **Manchester United** was not rich. A dog with a box around its neck had to collect money. The dog got lost. It was found by a rich man. He paid off all the team's debts. He became chairman and moved the club to Old Trafford.

- Brazil's first ever game was in 1914 against **Exeter**, who were in the country at the time.

Did you know?

Aston Villa, **Fulham**, **Everton**, **Barnsley** and **Bolton** football teams were all formed by their local church.

- In 1891 **Everton** fell out with the owner of their ground. They went to play somewhere else. The landlord put together a new team. He called them **Liverpool**.

- Italian club **AC Milan** was formed by an Englishman in 1889. They were called Milan Cricket and Football Club to start with.

- **Manchester City, Charlton** and **Birmingham** all play on grounds that used to be rubbish dumps.

- 20,000 people watched the first game to use floodlights. It was at **Sheffield United's** Bramhall Lane. Only 12,000 paid. The rest sneaked in – the gates and fences were not lit up!

Crazy Quiz

Why do **Juventus** play in black and white stripes?

(answers on page 32)

Record breakers

Records are made to be broken. Do you think anyone will ever beat these records?

In 1999, **Manchester United** had the best season an English club has ever had. They won:

- the Premier League
- the FA Cup
- the European Champions' Cup.

The longest ever game was between **Stockport** and **Doncaster** in 1946. It took 203 minutes!

Why?

It was a cup match. The rules were different then. If it was a draw after 90 minutes, they had to play on until someone scored.

What happened?

The score was 2–2 after 90 minutes. They played on but were very tired. Some fans went home for tea and came back again! The referee stopped the game when players started to lie down.

And then?

Doncaster won the replay 4–0!

- The best start to a season is 29 games without losing. **Leeds** did it in 1973–74. **Liverpool** did it in 1987–88. Make up your own mind who was best. Here are their records:

	played	won	drawn	lost	for	against
Leeds	29	19	10	0	51	16
Liverpool	29	22	7	0	67	13

- **Chelsea** won a match 21–0! They beat a team from Luxembourg 8–0 away and 13–0 at home.

Crazy Quiz

Which goalkeeper went for the longest time before letting in a goal?

(answers on page 32)

Ups and downs

There are good times and bad times in football. And they can come all at once!

- **Manchester City** were First Division champions in 1936–37. Next season they were relegated! This is the only time this has ever happened.

- **Chester** waited 44 years for their first promotion.

- The 1985 League Cup Final was between **Norwich** and **Sunderland**. Both teams were relegated from the top division that season. **Norwich** won 1–0.

- In 1977 **Wimbledon** was a non-league team. By 1986 it was in the top division.

- Four teams have reached the FA Cup Final and been relegated in the same year:

    - **Manchester City** (1926)
    - **Leicester City** (1969)
    - **Brighton and Hove Albion** (1983)
    - **Middlesbrough** (1997)

To make it worse, they all lost the Cup Final! **Middlesbrough** even lost in the League Cup Final in 1997 too!

- **Arsenal** has been in the top division for the longest time, since 1919. But they should not be there at all. They never won promotion. They were just asked if they wanted to go up!

- In 1928 the top division was very close. **Derby** had 44 points and finished 4th. **Middlesbrough** had 37 points, and finished bottom!

- The fastest rise and fall:

This means to go from the bottom division to the top, then right back down again! **Northampton** and **Swansea** both did it in only nine seasons.

- **Northampton** 1960–69
- **Swansea** 1977–86

At least the fans could not say they were bored!

Daft debuts

A debut (*day-bew*) is when someone plays their first game for a team. Some players have had very unlikely debuts…

- Alan Shearer scored a hat-trick on his debut for **Southampton**. He was only 17.

- Barrie Jones of **Notts County** scored on his debut too. After six seconds!

- Keith Bertschin scored on his debut before kicking the ball. He came on as a sub for **Norwich**. The first thing he did was score with a header!

Did you know?

Alan Shearer has scored on his debut for every team he has ever played with.

- **Birmingham** goalkeeper Tony Coton saved a penalty on his debut. After 30 seconds!

- **Halifax** goalkeeper Stan Milto did not have such a happy debut. **Stockport** put 13 goals past him.

Whoops!

- The most amazing debut ever? It must be Henry Morris. He scored on his debut for Scotland. You might think lots of people have done that. But this man got a hat-trick ... in four minutes! Scotland won 8–2, but never picked Morris to play again!

Potty players

Football players do all sorts of odd things.

- When he got married, George Graham was an **Arsenal** player. His best man was Terry Venables, a **Spurs** player at the time. Three hours later they played each other. **Arsenal** won 4–0 and George Graham scored.

- A bit strange…

Mike England **(Spurs)** played for Wales!
Eric Welsh **(Torquay)** played for Ireland!
Laurie Scott **(Arsenal)** played for Ireland!
Alan Brazil **(Ipswich)** played for Scotland!
John Scott **(Grimsby)** played for N. Ireland!

- England player Paul Ince will only put on his shirt when he is running out on to the pitch.

- **Chelsea** goalkeeper Willie 'Fatty' Foulke was 6ft 3in tall and weighed over 20 stone.

- England striker Les Ferdinand once went on loan to a Turkish side. When he got there, a goat had its head cut off. The blood was wiped on Ferdinand's boots to bring him good luck!

- Spanish goalkeeper Zamora hated dirt. He took a brush on to the pitch to sweep the penalty area!

- Two **Leicester** players once scored half a goal each. They kicked the ball at the same time… into their own net!

Crazy Quiz

Arsenal goalkeepers never play in brand new shirts. Why not?

(answers on page 32)

- **Gillingham** bought a striker called Tony Cascarino. They paid for him with 13 tracksuits!

- Roberto di Matteo signed for **Chelsea** from **Lazio**. The **Lazio** fans said goodbye by smashing up his car. They do this for players they <u>like</u>!

- **Luton** once had a goalkeeper called Bywater. Their full-backs were named Lake and Beach!

- A **Stoke** player once spent 10 minutes of a match on his hands and knees. He was looking for a contact lens!

> **Did you know?**
>
> **York** once had a big letter 'Y' on their shirts. They changed it when people started calling them the 'Y-Fronts!'

Football families

- Brothers Bobby and Jack Charlton won the World Cup with England in 1966.

- Ian Bowyer and son Gary both played in the same **Hereford** team in 1990.

- Brothers Danny, Ray and Rod Wallace all played in the same **Southampton** side in 1989.

- Phil and Gary Neville both play for **Manchester United** and England. Their sister Tracey also plays for England … at netball!

- Eider Gudjohnsen was a sub for Iceland. He came on for his dad, Arnar!

Off you go!

Things don't always go very well…

- **Sheffield United** goalkeeper Kevin Pressman was sent off after 13 seconds. The first game of the season too!

- Vinnie Jones got booked after three seconds of a game. He was playing for **Chelsea**.

Vinnie and Gazza.

- The dirtiest game ever must be **Boca Juniors** v **Sporting Cristal** in Argentina. Nineteen players were sent off after a punch-up. Sixteen were sent to prison for a month! The three players not sent to prison were 'let off' … they were in hospital!

- Mick Flanagan and Derek Hales were sent off for fighting. They both played for the same team – **Charlton Athletic**!

- **Aberdeen** player Dean Windass was sent off three times in the same match!

1   Two bookings meant he was sent off.
2   Swearing at the ref on the way off got him a second red card.
3   Throwing the corner flag got him a third sending off.

Crazy Quiz

Which British player has been sent off the most times?

(answers on page 32)

Goofy goals

And it only takes a second to score one.

- By the end of the 1986 season, Ian Rush had scored in 120 games for **Liverpool**. They never lost any of them, winning 101 and drawing 19.

- A Brazil player scored after three seconds. After the kick-off he shot from the halfway line and scored. He had seen that the goalkeeper was still saying his prayers!

- Scottish team **Arbroath** won a game 36–0. And they had seven goals disallowed for offside!

Crazy Quiz

Who scored seven goals in one game and still lost?

(answers on page 32)

- The longest ever penalty shoot-out was between two teams in Argentina. After 44 penalties, the score finished at 20–19!

- **Manchester United** were losing 2–1. With 30 seconds to go, goalkeeper Peter Schmeichel went up for a corner. He scored – 2–2!

- Other goalkeepers have scored too. Peter Shilton scored from a goal kick. It bounced straight over the other goalie's head! **Leeds** keeper Gary Sprake even threw the ball into his own net.

- A goalie from Paraguay is his team's top scorer. He takes all the penalties and free kicks!

- A **Chesterfield** keeper put the ball down for a free kick. But the whistle had come from the crowd. A striker ran up and smacked the ball in the net!

Stunning results

When you hear these results, you can't believe your ears.

- **Manchester City** beat **Burnley** 8–3. Two days later **City** lost 8–3 to **Sheffield United**!

- **Leeds** and **Cardiff** were drawn against each other in the FA Cup in 1956, 1957 and 1958. All three games were at **Leeds**. All three were won by **Cardiff**. All three finished with a score of 2–1!

- There has only ever been one 6–6 draw in the league. It was between **Leicester** and **Arsenal**.

Did you know?

The only time the FA Cup has left England was in 1927. It was won by Cardiff, from Wales.

- **Everton** once won seven games in a row, with scores of 9–3, 8–1, 7–2, 9–2, 5–1, 5–0 and 4–2.

- Not so much fun if you support **Luxembourg** though. They played 80 times before they won a game. They also hold the record for the most defeats in a row – 32!

- In 1989 **Liverpool** thrashed **Crystal Palace** 9–0. Later that season **Palace** knocked **Liverpool** out of the FA Cup 4–3.

- The biggest score in the league was when **Tranmere** beat **Oldham** 13–4!

- **Villa** once drew 2–2 with **Leicester**. The same **Villa** player scored all four goals!

Crazy Quiz

Who lost a match on the way to the final but still won the FA Cup?

(answers on page 32)

- An Italian team did not lose a game all season. They still did not win the league!

- **Fulham** lost 10–0 to **Liverpool** in the first leg of a cup match. There was a programme for the second leg. **Fulham** printed what would happen if the scores were level at the end!

- **Bradford City** won two games in three days by the same score – 8–0!

- The worst ever start to a season was made by **Manchester United**. They lost their first 12 games in a row.

> **Did you know?**
>
> 'The Double' means winning the Premiership and the FA Cup in the same season. Manchester United are the only team to do this twice – a double Double!

- **Cambridge** played 12 home games in a row without letting in a goal. Then they let in four in six minutes in a game against **Oldham**!

- This 'goal' knocked England out of the World Cup. Diego Maradona scored it. Many people called him a cheat. Argentina went on to win the World Cup.

Maradona said this goal was helped by the 'Hand of God'.

The greatest fightbacks ever?

- Two teams from South America were playing in the cup. One side was losing 3–1. They were also down to nine men. Then they had two more players sent off. With five minutes left, they scored twice and drew the game 3–3 – with only seven players!

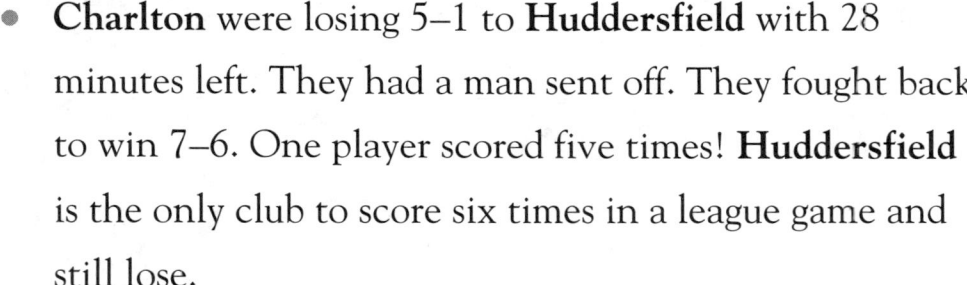

- **Charlton** were losing 5–1 to **Huddersfield** with 28 minutes left. They had a man sent off. They fought back to win 7–6. One player scored five times! **Huddersfield** is the only club to score six times in a league game and still lose.

Did you know?
Pele holds the record for scoring the most goals in one season – 126!

Extra time

Some things are so daft you can't explain them…

- In a match in Brazil the referee was sent off! He punched a player who was rude to him!

- A team from Iceland called a game off. Their ground was buried under lava from a volcano.

- German fans can be buried in special 'club-coffins.' Each coffin is made in the team colours and has the club badge on it.

- A Swedish player once missed a penalty so badly that it went out for a throw-in!

- A game in Africa was held up by killer bees. The bees were not after the players but went straight after the ref and the linesmen!

- When China played Greece, the teams lined up for the national anthems. They both thought they were listening to the other team's anthem. In fact a toothpaste advert was played by mistake!

Kevin Keegan and John Toshack get ready to be managers.

- **Barnsley's** ground had a pair of swing doors leading on to the pitch. Players always charged head-first through them. This stopped when the doors jammed and a player knocked himself out!

- A game once kicked off without a ref! Someone in the crowd blew a whistle when the players were ready to start. It was only when the ball went out of play that anyone noticed.

- A **Crystal Palace** player once got injured eating dinner before a game. A fish-bone stuck in his throat and he was taken to hospital!

Did you know?

Dennis Bergkamp hates flying. He always uses trains and boats when his team play in Europe.

Crazy Quiz – Answers

Why do Juventus play in black and white stripes? (page 7)
Because **Notts County** lent them a set of their shirts. Before this, **Juventus** played in pink shirts!

Which goalkeeper went for the longest time before letting in a goal? (page 10)
Chris Woods of **Rangers**. He did not let in a goal for 1,196 minutes. That's nearly 20 hours of football!

Arsenal goalkeepers never play in brand new shirts. Why not? (page 17)
Arsenal lost in the 1927 FA Cup Final to **Cardiff**. The **Arsenal** goalkeeper blamed his shiny new shirt. He said the ball slipped off his chest into the net. No **Arsenal** keeper has ever worn a brand new shirt since.

Which British player has been sent off the most times? (page 21)
Willie Johnstone. Fifteen times!

Who scored seven goals in one game and still lost? (page 22)
Denis Law. He scored six times for **Man. City** against **Luton**. The match was called off for bad weather. Law scored in the replay, but **City** lost 3–1!

Who lost a match on the way to the final but still won the FA Cup? (page 25)
Charlton. In 1946 the semi-finals were played over two legs. **Charlton** lost 2–1 away but won 3–1 at home.